Every Day's a Holiday

DEAN KOONTZ
Every Day's a Holiday

Amusing Rhymes
for Happy Times

Illustrated by PHIL PARKS

HarperCollins Publishers

Library of Congress Cataloging-in-Publication Data.
Koontz, Dean R. (Dean Ray).
Every day's a holiday : amusing rhymes for happy times / Dean Koontz ;
illustrated by Phil Parks.– 1st ed.   p.   cm.   Includes index.
Summary: An illustrated collection of poems celebrating holidays, including
real ones such as Easter, imaginary ones such as Gravity Day, international ones
such as Cinco de Mayo, and not-quite-holidays such as snow days.
ISBN 0-06-008584-3 – ISBN 0-06-008585-1 (lib. bdg.)
1. Holidays–Juvenile poetry. 2. Children's poetry, American. [1. Holidays–Poetry.
2. Humorous poetry. 3. American poetry.] I. Parks, Phil, ill. II. Title.
PS3561.O55E94 2003   811'.54–dc21   2003000506

Typography by Carla Weise
1 2 3 4 5 6 7 8 9 10
❖
First Edition

To Gerda, who makes me so happy
that I'm always in the mood to write funny verse
—D.K.

For my family,
Cynthia, Joel, Amanda and Beth,
who make every day a day to celebrate
—P.P.

CONTENTS

Every Day's a Holiday

HOLIDAY GIFTS

Many holidays require that you give a gift,
Something fine, fun, and sparkly, if you get my drift.
But that gets expensive if you're tight with a buck.
Therefore, here are some clever suggestions. Good luck!

Why not give your sister a big box of rock salt?
Then tell her that she has not one tiniest fault.
And tell her that she is the SALT OF THE EARTH,
So no other gift could match her true worth.

Give your friend bottled water from the kitchen sink,
Then tell him deep down in your heart you think
That in this world full of worry and strife,
Friendship like his is the WATER OF LIFE!

Of course *you* will receive a box of wet crud,
Because from now on YOUR NAME WILL BE MUD!

STOP THE WORLD!
IT'S YOUR BIRTHDAY!

The day that you were born, the sun spun in the sky.

Not.

The day that you were born, the cows grew wings to fly.

Not.

On that day of your birth, the moon came out bright pink.

Not.

On that day of your birth, all skunks refused to stink.

Not.

When you arrived on Earth, poets ran out of rhyme.

Not.

When you arrived on Earth, the clocks ran out of time.

Not.

The day that you were born, your family did rejoice.

True.

The day that you were born, you had a squeaky voice.

True.

On that day of your birth, nobody really knew,

(*Wait*)

On that day of your birth, that you would be so *you*.

True.

When you arrived on Earth, you had done nothing yet.

True.

When you arrived on Earth, not one goal had you set.

True.

The world will never stop to celebrate your day.

(*Wait*)

But if you're kind to friends and kind to strangers, too,

(*Wait*)

Your name will raise a smile, and everyone will say,

(*Patience*)

"This whole world *ought* to stop and make a bow to you."

HOLIDAY DATA GLITCH

On New Year's Eve the Easter Bunny
Delivered eggs and birthday money.
Valentine's Day, the reindeer all came
—Donner, Blitzen, and Cupid by name.
Santa with gifts, showed some confusion.
He seemed to suffer from a delusion
That Christmastime had come 'round again
In just two months. He made our heads spin.
On July Fourth, the goblins arrived,
Witches, monsters. Somehow we survived.

On Thanksgiving, fireworks were a bad sign.
And the turkey sang out, "Auld Lang Syne."
On our birthdays we got things Irish green.
The birthday cake came on Halloween.
"The Holiday Management Elves have fumbled,"
Santa Claus to his weary reindeer grumbled.
"We celebrated May First all July long.
Their brand-new computer has everything wrong."

NEW YEAR'S EVE

On every New Year's Eve they scold,
"Bring in the new, throw out the old!
What do we care for what is old?
Mold is old, nobody likes mold."

But please don't throw my grandma out,
Even if Grandma has the gout.
And I do really, truly doubt
That we should throw our old dog out.

Grandma bakes the bestest cookies.
Dog's my pal when I play hooky.
Grandma loves me and always will.
And we all love our old dog still.

Oh, must we burn our old house down?
And what about our nice old town?
And what about that nice old clown?
Should the elephant run him down?

Yes, I like new, but I like old,
As I like hot but also cold.
As I like sour, I like sweet.
I think old friends like you are neat.

NEW YEAR'S DAY

The time has come for New Year's resolutions,
For righting wrongs and making restitutions.
Let us now resolve to always tell the truth,
To shampoo our hair and brush our every tooth,
To eat spinach by the barrel, not ice cream,
To help every friend achieve a cherished dream.
Let's resolve to study harder every day,
To be loyal, brave, and selfless, come what may.

Or . . . let's resolve to eat tons of pie and cake,
To sun and swim all summer out at the lake,
To be as lazy as any sloth or slug,
To tease little children with an ugly bug.
Hey, this resolution business is a snap,
If you're able always to avoid the trap
Of resolving to do what's so hard to do,
And resolve instead to paint your sleeping sister blue.

APPROPRIATE HOLIDAY ENTERTAINMENT

Fireworks are always nice.

(Fireworks can be done twice.)

Sweet song and happy dance,

Horses that proudly prance,

Tigers leaping through hoops of fire,

Dogs strolling in formal attire,

Cats reciting free verse,

Waiters juggling bratwurst,

Elephants parading,

Tenors serenading,

Skaters figure skating,

Tumblers tumble-ating,
Ranks of fiddlers fiddling,
Drummers paradiddling,
Many riddlers riddling,
Ten big niddlers niddling—
These forms of fun are fine.
Not one is out of line.
But if you eat until you spew,
That simply will not do.
And if the gathered guests you moon,
You'll be in trouble real soon.

CARNIVAL!

Through the streets of Rio de Janeiro,
Singing as sweet as the happy sparrow,
And dancing the samba from dusk to dawn,
Partying till the last of night is gone,
People celebrate the four days before Lent,
Forgetting worries about bills and rent.
On the fantastic fourth and final night,
Dressed with flowers, carrying candles bright,
They parade on the beach, then into the ocean,
To honor Iemanja with their samba motion.
Iemanja is the goddess of the sea,
Symbolizing freedom and liberty.
When Carnival's over, Brazilians sleep.
Like a hibernating bear, they sleep deep.
To me this holiday sounds really neat—
Unless you're the guy who must sweep the street!

GRAVITY DAY

I'm a good friend to gravity
And gravity's a friend to me.
Oh, it holds me to the planet,
Along with trees and rocks of granite.
Without it I would float away
Like a balloon on a spring day.
I would float high and higher still,
Above the river and the hill,
Above the mountain, into space,
Where meteors would smack my face,
Where my poor body would explode.
I'd look just like a truck-squashed toad.
We ought to praise gravity every day,
Not just on the date that calendars say.
I don't know about you, but as for me,
I'll always be a friend of gravity.

MARTIN LUTHER KING, JR. DAY

He taught us that right is better than wrong.

He knew that love can make you strong.

He knew that truth is all you need

To grow sweet freedom from a seed.

He taught that all of us can be

Anything that we want to be.

SNOW DAY

Oh, what a sight!
It snowed last night!
Oh, what a thrill!
White glen, white hill.
White tree, white street.
So cold, no heat.
Big drifts, much ice.
Froze cat, froze mice,
Froze you, froze me,
Froze lake, froze tree.
Broken branches.

Avalanches!
It's snowing still,
And still it will.
Higher, higher!
Telephone wire.
Higher, higher,
And still higher!
All the city,
What a pity,
Lost deep in snow,
And still more snow.

Froze my big toe.
It had to go.
I cut it off.
I've got a cough.
I just heard, dude,
We're out of food.
We're gonna starve.
We'll have to carve
Those frozen mice.
They won't taste nice.

But better that
Than carve the cat.
And better, too,
Than carving you.
It's a wizard
of a blizzard!
Love snow, I do,
I do, it's true.
I'm not a fool—
They've canceled school!

VALENTINE'S DAY

"No young man may marry.
No Tom, Dick, or Larry,"
Said Roman Emperor Claudius Two.

"Soldiers fight better with arrows and knives
When they've no families—no kids, and no wives,"
Said Roman Emperor Claudius Two.

A priest named Valentine would not obey,
And married young couples, day after day.
"Throw him in prison!" said Claudius Two.

Children loved Valentine, priest of good cheer,
And brought him cards that said, *Please do not fear.*
Mothers and fathers loved Valentine, too,
And brought him cards that said, *Please don't be blue.*
They dropped letters through the bars of his cell.
And to honor him, each church rang its bell.

"I am the emperor, all must obey!
Execute Valentine this very day!"
Said Roman Emperor Claudius Two.

February 14, 269,
They executed good Saint Valentine,
To please the emperor, Claudius Two.

Now centuries later, we like to say,
"Be my Valentine," on that special day.
But who remembers old Claudius Two?

ABRAHAM LINCOLN'S BIRTHDAY

Abe was born in a humble log cabin.

He walked FIVE LONG MILES every day to school!

I guess he was mentally unbalanced.

But the log cabin part sounds kinda cool.

GEORGE WASHINGTON'S BIRTHDAY

The Father of our Country

Chopped down a cherry tree.

Thanks to my reputation,

Mother will no doubt blame me.

SAINT PATRICK'S DAY

Saint Patrick now we celebrate.

You don't need to be Irish, mate,

To say that old Saint Pat was great.

From Ireland he drove all the snakes.

Drove them from fields and woods and lakes,

All by himself, for goodness sakes!

Of snakes, Saint Pat left Ireland clean,

And did it without being mean.

He drove them in a limousine.

It was a sleek and lovely car,
With a television and a bar.
He drove them fast and very far.

Often the snakies took a nap,
And never understood the trap.
Pat drove them to another land
And left them sunning on the sand.

He left the reptiles free to roam,
Knowing they could never crawl home.
Saint Pat was clever, not a sap.
He knew that snakes can't read a map.

THE FIRST DAY
OF SPRING

Deep in the cave

The old bear wakes.

No growl, no rave.

He yawns and shakes.

His dreams are done.

He snorts and blinks.

It's time for fun.

But now he stinks.

Winter slid past

While he just dozed.

He needs soap fast.

Keep your nose closed.

EVERY DAY'S A HOLIDAY

When you say, "Have a nice day," I grin with delight.
Did you think I was planning a day full of fright?
Who wouldn't rather eat cake, and receive a gift rose,
Than eat dead-worm pudding or cut off his sweet nose?

"My friend, have a nice day!" you declare with a smile,
So perhaps I'll avoid that big mean crocodile,
Won't leap among rattlesnakes heaped in a high pile,
Or jump off a tall tree and fall half a mile.

So I'll have a nice day, after which I just might
Also decide to enjoy a super nice night.
I'll sleep on a soft bed, not on old rusty nails,
And snack on cookies, instead of raw runny snails.

Some days can be nothing but bleak and bad,

Nothing but grumpy and dumpy and sad.

But more days than not, a person can choose,

To win and be happy, not to be sad and lose.

Every day is a holiday here in our happy house.

Some days we toast the purring cat, some days the squeaky mouse.

We insist on sweet laughter, on kindness, not strife,

And celebrate good will, good deeds, and love—our happy life.

EASTER:

THE DANGER OF IMPROVING
HOLIDAY TRADITIONS

It's time to retire the Easter Bunny.
He's not exciting; he's not even funny.
He wears no mask or cape. He doesn't fly.
He's not a superhero or a master spy.
He doesn't have the degree of glamour
For which modern audiences clamor.

An Easter Cow wouldn't be much better.

An Easter Turtle would be no go-getter.

An Easter Eagle might be just the thing,

Zooming here to there with zip and zing.

An Easter Dog might be the best of all.

A Great Dane. A chihuahua is too small.

To deliver candy, a dog has no ambition,

So to get him hip to the tradition,

We'll fix floppy rabbit ears on his head,

Or put him in a rabbit suit instead.

Give him a sporty Easter Dogmobile

With a laser cannon and wings of steel!

Let's forget the candy altogether.

Make him a hero who fights bad weather!

Easter Dog versus the fierce hurricane!

Easter Dog, who tames the wind, the rain!

And he'll need a trusty sidekick, of course.

In another bunny suit: the Easter Horse!

APRIL FOOL'S DAY

WARNING: *A new federal law requires that anyone who tries to fool another on the first day of April, but fails to do so, will be sent to April Fool's Training Camp for sixty days to undergo the vigorous exercise of his or her silliness gene. Furthermore, anyone who is fooled by a prankster but refuses to admit being fooled will simply be beaten senseless with sturdy plastic bags full of warm oatmeal. This is a cruel law, but necessary. Meanwhile, here are some suggested harmless lies for this holiday.*

This morning men from Mars landed in France!

They look somewhat like bears, somewhat like ants.

They wear huge rubber shoes and checkered pants.

They drink root beer, speak Dutch, and love to dance.

You know that nasty kid in Ms. Smith's class?
The one who makes fun and who likes to sass,
And went to London on a bathroom pass?
He just exploded from bad lunchroom gas.

Don't move! Don't! Hold still! A big deadly bug
Is perched upon your head and looking smug.
I'll smash it with this heavy cider jug
Or this board. Trust me, I'll get that bad bug!

Pssssst! On your chin you have a drip of drool.
At lunch we're having monkey meat and gruel.
The principal hired a pro wrestler who'll
Body slam any kid who breaks a rule.

SAKURA MATSUKI
(CHERRY BLOSSOM FESTIVAL)

Can you say *Saw-koo-raw Mot-soo-key?*
Oh, come on! It's really not spooky.
In Japan we go to "hana-mi,"
To "look at the flowers," don't you see?
Cherry trees all blossom in the spring,
Each a lovely pink and fragrant thing.
We picnic, play under blooming trees,
Drink sake, make merry, sometimes sneeze.
Japan has four hundred varieties:
Cherry trees, cherry trees, cherry trees!
Cherry trees in Japan, however,
Bear no fruit, no cherries, no, never.
This is all true, and you can trust me:
Cherryless, cherry-free, cherry trees.
So on your back, mouth open to the sky,
You will not receive free cherry pie.
Just blossoms, just leaves, meet your big grin.
A few bugs may also fall right in.

DINO DAY

We decorate our house this day each year
And greet one another with great good cheer.
We laugh and dance and sing and make merry,
For without this holiday, life would be scary.
We eat cakes and cookies, we're all well fed,
As we celebrate that the dinosaurs are dead.
We feel no sadness for that long-gone scaly bunch,
Because if they were here they would eat us for lunch.

Imagine a dinosaur in a nice dino diner,
Serving up food that couldn't be finer.
He might order a baked Barbara, a fricasseed Fred,
A side order of Sammy slaw, one Lucy (just the head),
A big bowl of Lou stew, and what he likes the most—
Six scowling school principals grilled on toast.

CINCO DE MAYO

Now here comes Cinco de Mayo,

From Alaska to the bayou.

In Maine, Florida, and Ohio,

Folks are having pico de gallo,

Celebrating the French defeat,

Eating treat after fancy treat,

'Cause Mexico once kicked the pants

Of an army that came from France.

I know the year it happened, but do you?

Those pants got kicked in 1862.

TEACHER'S DAY

On teacher's day it is well understood
That we should be polite and very good.
We should listen with strictest attention
To every word our teacher may mention.
We should not sneak a big frog into class.
We should not whisper, we must never sass.
We should learn well and do all of our work.
We should not call any classmate a jerk.

Our teacher says this day has
One thousand hours in it.
We are quite sure, however,
It lasts less than a minute.

ANNUAL ANIMALS' DAY
IN COURT

Did you know that once every year
Animals have a right to hear
And be heard in a court of law,
If they swear truth on upraised paw,
Or hoof or claw? And do not spit
Or run around, just calmly sit?

JUDGE BOULLE

They show up each year without fail.
And may send you—or me—to jail.
To animals this is a holiday,
For it brings a little justice their way.

No poor toad can really cause a bad wart.
You can't take tiny toads to civil court,
And then expect to win piles of money
For that weird growth that looks awful funny.
So toads will work up a righteous dander
If you should persist in this vile slander.
They'll sue you for your last shiny penny,
Even if you don't have all that many.

Pigs! Pigs are not a filthy bunch.

They don't prefer garbage for lunch.

Their snort is in fact a *wuffle*,

And they like a tasty truffle.

They lie in mud just to stay cool.

They don't *have* air-conditioned school.

In court they'll swear on a Bible

That you've committed dirty libel.

Bats! Bats don't nest in human hair.
Your curly locks they won't ensnare.
Hair gel, hair spray just makes 'em puke,
Whether you're a king, queen, or duke.
They do not want to suck your blood.
They'd rather eat a pile of mud.
Your lies they so much do detest,
And will march in noisy protest.

Wolves! Wolves do not eat little kids

And scoop their brains out through their lids.

They don't dress up like your grandma

To lie and sneak on slippered paw.

If you make these accusations

And antiwolf proclamations,

They will not go to court and shout—

They'll simply rip your guts right out.

Wolves like juries, judges, and court,

But at the sight of a lawyer, they snort.

To you, Animals' Day in Court might seem

Less like a holiday than a bad dream.

But the animals look forward all year,

To bending—not biting!—a judge's ear.

MOTHER'S DAY IS EVERY DAY, THANKS TO US

Yes, we do so much for our mothers,

More than we do for any others.

We never pick up our dirty clothes,

A habit mother totally loathes.

We always leave our rooms a big mess,

But just out of love, we now confess.

We eat much like the Missing Link.
We pile dishes high in the sink.
We track black mud. We spill blue ink.
We sass and grouch before we think.

We lie to her without a blink.
We bring home things that ooze and slink.
We do so much for our mothers,
More than we do for all others.

Why do we do this, do you suppose?
Oh, every child the true answer knows.
We know poor Mother would be so blue,
If she didn't have something to do!

CAT DAY

Today's the day we honor every cat.

(Not that any cat cares about any of that.)

Today's the day we rave about their fur.

(Although quiet is what any cat would prefer.)

We acclaim their genius at catching mice.

(While the bored cat stretches, sighs, then yawns twice.)

We admire their cool, calm self-reliance.

(While any cat puts more stock in its defiance.)

We celebrate their limberness and speed.

(But any cat's opinion of itself is all it needs.)

MEMORIAL DAY

Now we honor the memory
Of those who died to keep us free,
To spare us pain and misery.
They died for us and liberty.
For all we have or ever might,
We owe them every day and night.
We mourn their deaths but celebrate
The bravery that made them great.
They went to war, they went away,
That we might sing and laugh and play.

THINGS THAT CAN SPOIL
A GOOD HOLIDAY

A gum boil the size of a basketball.
A hundred-pound spider in the front hall.
Rattlesnakes rattling inside of the wall.
Werewolves rampaging at the shopping mall.
Being chased by a sharp-toothed devil doll.
That's bad enough, but that isn't all.

Falling off the roof onto a porcupine.

Meeting a cannibal ready to dine.

Chased by a pack of hungry swine.

Pickled to death in a huge vat of brine.

Snared by a slithering man-eating vine.

Having eight arrows when the deer has nine.

Oh, that's not even a little of it.

Encountering elephants in a snit.

Sitting where a gorilla wants to sit.

Angering a bear that's ready to spit.

Tumbling in a wild cockapoodle pit.

Failing to move when a rhino says "Git!"

But the holiday spoiler that makes me scream

Is Mom forgetting to buy ice cream!

FATHER'S DAY

I'm glad for Dad,

Even when I'm bad,

Even when I'm mean,

Even when I'm green

With envy or

I've tracked the floor

With filthy muck,

Or when I chuck

My little brother

At my mother.

I'm glad for Dad,

Even when he's mad

About this or that,

About the cat

I zipped inside my sister's purse.

Oh, I've done worse.

When I've been bad,

I'm glad for Dad,

For his stern voice

At my bad choice.

Dad says because of me he's losing his hair.

Watching him go bald, I know he must care.

THE EIGHTEEN ACCEPTABLE EXCUSES NOT TO CELEBRATE A HOLIDAY

You're dumb.

You're numb.

You're ill.

You're swill.

You're mean.

Not clean.

You're mad.

You're bad.

Clueless.

Mooless. *

Toothless.

Ruthless.

Useless.

Mooseless. **

You're white

With blight.

You're green

With spleen.

In bed

Or dead. **

*   A fit excuse only for cows.
** A fit excuse only if you are a moose
    who happens to be alone on a holiday.
*** Not a fit excuse on Día de los Muertos
    or Halloween.

TOAD DAY

A toad is usually little,

All legs and head, not much middle.

He hops and leaps.

He sometimes peeps.

Your heart he'll win

With his sweet grin.

He eats skeeters, beetles, and flies,

Which doesn't seem entirely wise.

Yet this diet works well for him.

He never ever finds it grim.

He never thinks it's bland.

In fact he thinks it's grand.

Without his special appetite,

Our world would simply not be right.

We would have to eat the flies

And beetles and skeeters baked in pies.

If ever an evening were to sound right,

You and I would have to *ribbit* all night.

On Toad Day we celebrate,

For the toad is truly great.

It may be warty, it may be so very small,

But the toad is the toadiest creature of all.

THE LAST DAY OF SCHOOL,
THE SADDEST DAY OF THE YEAR

Gee whiz, this is
The day! Hooray!
We're free! Hee, hee.
No ABCs.
No test, we rest.
Today we play!
We're free! Hee, hee.
No XYZs.
No teacher's wrath
When we fail math.
No words to spell,
No chalk to smell.
No lunchroom food
To spoil our mood.
No bathroom pass
for lunchroom gas.
We're free! We're free!
Buzz like a bee!
We're loose, we're loose!
Honk like a goose!
We're out of here!
Run like a deer!

GRADUATION DAY

One day Rod Clod will graduate from school.

He cannot think of anything more cool.

Once he's gotten his graduation ring,

Clod will refuse to learn another thing.

He says he will refuse even to think.

Into a pit of ignorance he will sink,

Until he is as dumb as any tree.

He says this with a certain grinning glee.

He also thinks he's a fascinating guy.

But I can't for the life of me think why.

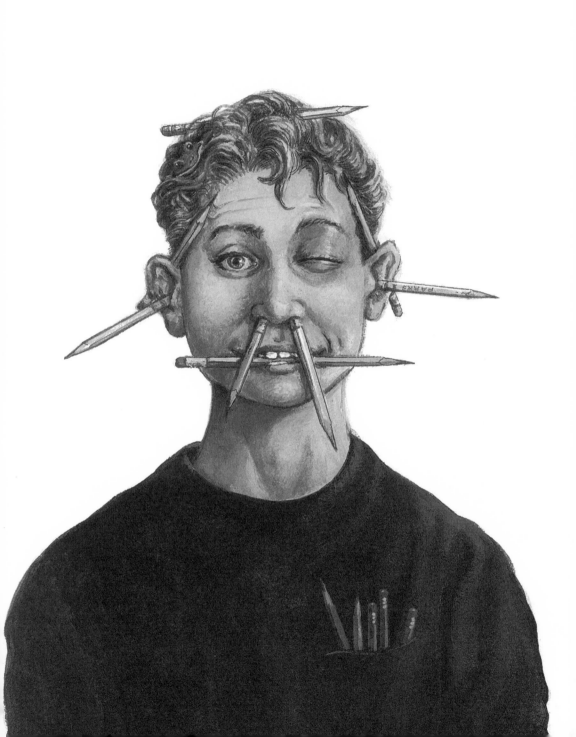

THE FIRST DAY OF SUMMER

The bear seeks the honey.
Then the bees seek the bear.
And here's something funny—
They can't sting through his hair.
They celebrate summer hours,
The old bear and the bees alike.
Bees will caper in the flowers;
The grinning bear will ride his bike.
This long summer will be enjoyed
Also by children running free,
Assuming that they can avoid
The bite of bear, the sting of bee!

ME DAY

I'm going to start a Me Day.

You all will be charged a fee—say

A hundred dollars each—which may

Be given to me on my Me Day.

I want good stuff for free—okay?

All free for me on my Me Day.

I want you to shout, "Hip-hooray!"

Every hour on the hour on my Me Day.

Line up right here, right now, I say,

With your hundred bucks and your "Hip-hooray!"

At last it's time for me to have my way.

I'm rested, I'm ready for my Me Day.

INDEPENDENCE DAY:
FREE TO BE IGNORANT OLD ME

Since 1776—Hooray!—
We've celebrated Independence Day,
Beginning with the Evolutionary War
That we fought in 1744.
Determined to be forever free,
We won our freedom from Germany.
George Washington led our troops,
Who ate jelly toast and Froot Loops.
Perhaps General Washington gave a holler
When he threw a shiny silver dollar
Across somebody's Pontiac.
I guess somebody threw it back.

We declared the equality of all people

And said any church can build a steeple.

We said everybody has certain rights

Except on certain Wednesday nights.

Among those rights are life, liberty,

Free doughnuts, hats, and dignity.

My teacher says with this poor knowledge,

I'll have to *fight* my way into college.

And teacher says we can only stay free

If we know the true source of our liberty.

If I've made mistakes, I just don't see.

Perhaps you could point them out to me?

DOG DAY

My dog has a nose that is black and cold,
And a heart as pure as the purest gold.
She loves to chase and fetch a tennis ball,
And runs to me, tail wagging, when I call.
Most dogs would rather smile than scowl or frown,
Because at heart each good dog is a clown.
Which is why I do solemnly declare
A holiday to praise dogs everywhere.

Oh, dogs are smarter than we think. It's true.

Smarter than me and smarter than you, too.

They arrived here on spaceships from a star

As far away as a star can be far.

They can spell, read books, do math, also talk.

They can levitate, have no need to walk.

They are genuises, generals, you see:

The super-secret kings of the galaxy.

So when my dog wants a long belly rub

—You better listen closely to me, bub—

I do what doggy wants, and so should you.

She has a mighty ray gun, this is true.

If I failed to rub her furry belly,

She might zap me to a pile of jelly.

Dogs can perform Shakespeare if they rehearse.

Dogs are the secret masters of the universe.

FRIENDSHIP DAY

I had a friend named Fred.

He was a plant

With lots of leaves, no head.

He didn't rant.

He never lied.

Fred never borrowed books.

He never cried.

Cared not about his looks.

On Friendship Day, I think of Fred,

With nothing in his nonexistent head.

He never spat

Or wore an ugly hat

Or behaved like a rat.

Fred was above all that.

Never shouted, either.

Was a quiet breather.

He listened well.

He'd never tell

Secrets to another.

He was like my brother.

Fred always did what's right,

Could not run from a fight.

I liked leafy old Fred, and yet . . .

Our friendship had to fade.

The truth I won't evade.

Fred would just set, and set, and set

On the table, on the flooring.

He never lied. He didn't rant.

He never cried. He was a plant.

Fred was boring, boring, boring.

HOLIDAYS ON OTHER PLANETS

The Martians' favorite day of the year
Is one we don't wish to celebrate here.
That special morning, they rise from their beds
And with curious instruments cut off their heads.
Each wraps its head with bright ribbons and bows
And gives it away to someone it knows.

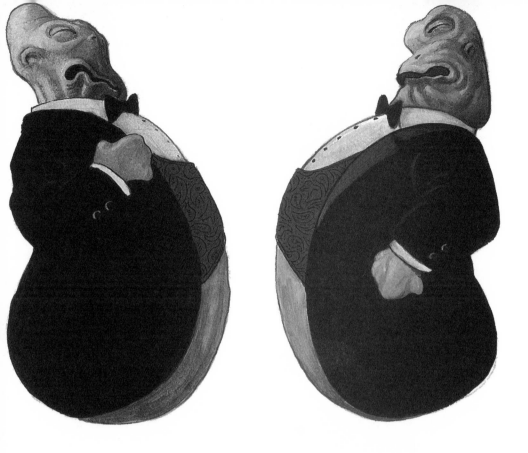

Each New Year's on Saturn,
The life forms bluster and blow.
They brag and they swagger,
They tell huge lies and crow.
They shoot off their big mouths,
Oh, they're so full of sass,
Because life forms on Saturn
Are huge bags of hot gas.

On the planet of Hurkle de Merkle
They all gickel with sherkle and ferkle.
They snooder, snidder, and sneeder so bright,
All through the green day and through the pink night.
And if you're confused or now full of mirth,
You're not a Hurkle de Merkle by birth.

On the planet known as Forgetful World
The flags are rolled up before they're unfurled.
Dinner is eaten when it's not been made.
Bills are paid though they've already *been* paid.
No one goes on holiday when they please,
Because they cannot find where they left the keys.
They put on party hats, but forget it's been done,
So they wear nine hats instead of just one.

On Pluto (also known as Planet Worm),

All things that live there do wriggle and squirm.

I know their holidays, but here's the trick:

The details would make you violently sick.

LABOR DAY

Work gives our lives dignity and meaning.

Yet here against my shovel I am leaning.

We must work if we wish to earn our keep.

But if you could earn mine, I wouldn't weep.

See, if I worked, *you* might not have a job.

You'd sit at home alone and sadly sob.

By staying home, I leave a job for you.

Oh, it's the very least that I could do.

I think that laziness gets a bad rap.

You celebrate. I'll go home and take a nap.

GRANDFATHER'S DAY

Robbie's a rhino. Grandpa is one, too.

Grandpa's the biggest creature in the zoo.

If on his grandson Grandpa ever sat,

Robbie'd be as flat as a sat-on hat.

Flat as a pancake with a tail and horn,

Flat as the flattest flatworm ever born.

Yet fear of flatness isn't the reason

That on Grandfather's day, every season,

Robbie's nice to Grandpa, who looms above.

The real reason, as you know, is simply love.

GRANDMA'S DAY *or*
WHY ONE DAY THERE WILL BE GOOD COOKIES ON THE MOON

Grandma is great!
Let's celebrate!

Without Grandma
I'd have no ma.
Without my ma
There'd be no me.
Without Granny
Where would I be?

My other grandma
Gave me my pa.
Without my pa
There'd be no me.
If I weren't me
Who would I be?

Might be a gnu
Stuck in a zoo.
Or one cuckoo
Stuck in a clock,
Or in a flock.
Might be a rock.

Or then, of course,
Might be a horse,
An old, old horse
Made into glue,
Or one blue shoe,
Or even two.

One day real soon
I'll write a tune
And buy the moon
To give Granny.
I love her, see,
Like she loves me.

THE FIRST DAY OF AUTUMN

All the green leaves turned color.
Then all the bright leaves fell down.
Sue gathered them, every one,
From every last tree in town.

She tied them to the branches,
Which required nearly a week,
Leaving her oh so weary,
And the trees still looked quite bleak.

Squirrels gathered fallen nuts

And stored them deep in the dark.

Sue took nuts from the squirrels

And returned them to the park.

When birds began to sing less

And made plans to fly far south,

She tried tying them to trees

Till they dropped worms in her mouth.

Spitting out the worms, Sue cried,

"My mind will soon just splinter!

Crack! Split! Explode! Go ba-ba-ba-*boom*!

I like autumn but hate the winter!"

LOST-TOOTH DAY

Tooth fairy, tooth fairy!
All children be wary!

Down the chimney he slides
Or through a window sneaks,
And under your pillow
The freaky fellow peeks.

He's searching for the tooth
You lost this afternoon.
He's the oddest oddball
This side of the moon.

For teeth he pays good money,
And will come back more than once.
Buying worthless teeth we've lost,
He might seem to be a dunce.

Now and then a foolish child,
Scheming hard to get rich quick,
Will pull out all his good teeth.
Oh, does this not make you sick?

Having bought one big mouthful,
The tooth fairy slinks away,
But this sly fellow figures
To return another day.

The poor foolish child soon learns
He can neither bite nor chew.
He discovers he can eat
Only liquid, mush, or goo.

Soon the fairy calls once more,
Selling old teeth for big dough.
The reckless child then buys back
Each shiny white dental row.

The price he must pay is high,
To regain his precious teeth.
When he pronounces *meatball*
It no longer sounds like "meeth."

Oh, celebrate Lost-Tooth Day,
But don't be a total fool.
Each greedy child will wind up
Mumbling toothlessly, with drool.

ROSH HASHANAH

Rosh Hashanah means "the head of the year,"
When those who've lived right have less to fear
Than those who've lived wrong. Oh, say, do you hear
Sounds of the shofar, that horn sweet and clear?
Its notes waken us to the bad we've done,

Though remembering our sins isn't much fun.
Today we are judged for what we have been,
As we prepare a new year to begin.
God sets our fortunes for the year ahead.
We who've lived wrong can't hide under the bed,
Hide in the closet or under the stairs.
Can't hide in a cave, but not because of bears.
So better live well and then celebrate,
For you will have earned a happier fate.
Dip bread in honey, eat sugary treats,
Pray for a year that will be good and sweet.

TROLL DAY, WHETHER YOU LIKE IT OR NOT

Under our bridges they sit and they wait
To gobble up girls and unwary boys
Who see these evil lurking beasts too late.
Their *crunchity munch* is such a vile noise.

Trolls terrorize dogs and old stray cats, too.
They chase our teachers, as swift as gazelles,
Though teachers taste sour and are hard to chew.
Trolls bake good children in sweet pastry shells.

Trolls eat mailmen with two dashes of salt.

They pepper grandmas and sugar rock stars,

Eat cops like peanuts, with chocolate malts.

"Canned meat," to most trolls, means people in cars.

Trolls have no manners, eat only with spoons.

They spit, but they don't spit in their spittoons.

They pick at their noses, pick at their feet,

And show you their boogers, *which they then eat!*

Why celebrate these hideous creatures,

With their gnarled and so fearsome features?

Well, I guess it's because, because, because . . .

Nobody, nobody, nobody else does.

YOM KIPPUR

This most hallowed day of the Jewish year
Is the time to make our bad consciences clear.
On this day of atonement, to make things right,
We fast from sundown until the next night.
God forgives all our offenses toward Him,
But He won't forgive those acts mean and grim
That we committed against Jane and Jim,
Against Morty, Paul, Joe, Rachel, and Tim.
We ask forgiveness of those we offend,
And with their pardons, our souls will soon mend.
I told my mother I'd wronged only one
All through the past year till this setting sun.

She reminded me how I teased poor Ben,

How I shoved Mina, how I laughed at Glenn,

How I'd been rude to Samuel and Sadie—

And other behavior that might seem shady!

Lunch money spent on cake, cookies, candy.

The lizard dropped on that girl named Sandy.

The skunk in the schoolroom, that joke with the hog.

And leashing my brother to that big old dog,

Then tying sausages to our fat old cat,

And turning them loose, and watching them scat.

If this past year seemed a whole lot of fun,

It wasn't funny when my mother was done.

To ask forgiveness from those I've done wrong,

This year Yom Kippur should be one year long!

HOLIDAY DINNER

You know you've had too much to eat

When you can't get up on your feet.

"You've lost control," Mother will sigh.

"You're covered with gravy and pie."

But manners are the least of your troubles,

For you can't find your cat, little Bubbles.

You're afraid the sweet furry Siamese

Was eaten after the turkey, before the cheese.

COLUMBUS DAY

Today we celebrate curiosity,
Courage, daring, and seamanship.
Columbus discovered America
After a long and miserable trip.
When he landed on these shores,
It was the Spanish flag he unfurled.
Then he had a fabulous time—
Two weeks at Disney World.

HOW TO GET TO SLEEP
BEFORE A HOLIDAY

When you're too excited to sleep,
You might try counting sheep.
Or perhaps let the sheep count you.
Sheep can count no higher than two.
They'll count you again and again,
For they're not very smart. And then
The sound of their droning voices
Will give you only two choices:
Go to sleep and do not complain
Or let them drive you slowly insane.

MR. HALLOWEEN

Of all the many holidays
And special days, and happy days,
Jinx likes this scary day the most.
He won't dress up as ghoul or ghost.
Won't dress as a devil, either,
Nor a dragony fire-breather.
Won't dress up as a vampire bat
Or as a creepy graveyard rat.
Jinx is a monster through and through.
He doesn't need costumes, like you.
All he needs is a bag for treats,
As at each door he loudly bleats,
"Candy is dandy, so is gum.
Oh, please, oh, please, oh, give me some!"

His costume wins the highest praise.
This night, being a monster pays.
His stash of candy quickly grows,
As on from house to house he goes,
Trailed by platoons of costumed kids
Who don't know what he really is.
He was created in a lab,
In a big vat, then on a slab,
Brewed, stewed, glued, and ventilated.
Then his brain was fabricated.
Kids like to travel in his pack,
Because each soon fills up a sack.
But now one thing we must disclose:
Take *his* candy . . . he'll eat your nose.

WHAT SHOULD GO INTO
A HOLIDAY PIE

Sugar and cinnamon,

Just as a minimum.

Coconut and custard,

Though please, please, no mustard.

Two pounds of chocolate chips

But very few toad lips.

Almonds and lemon curds,

Not twenty-four blackbirds.

One ounce of river mud,

Three drops of monkey blood,

Nose of a vampire bat,

One tail from a black cat,

A crocodile's big toe—

Whoa! Wait! That's not right! No!
I don't know how or why
My recipe for pie,
Got mixed up, through and through
With an old witches' brew.
Forget the river mud.
Substitute one cow cud.
Use no vampire bat's nose.
Instead use all its toes.
One golden crispy crust.
Finish with Dead Sea dust.

UNFORGETABLE
HOLIDAE
PYES
by
Baba yaga

HOLIDAE PIES YAGA

PRAISE FOR
TWILIGHT PIES

PIES OF DARKNESS

FROM THE CORNER
OF HIS PIE

SUGA

CINN

PARK
MONK
BLOO

DÍA DE LOS MUERTOS

From north Mexico to the Yucatán,

Every woman, each child, and every man

Welcomes and honors the beloved dead,

Telling stories of what they did and said

When they lived in this world, not in the next.

Each family believes that it detects

The presence of those who were lost to death,

Here once more, as invisible as breath.

This day departed souls return to earth.

We welcome them with dancing and with mirth,

With all their favorite foods and much to drink.
We can half hear their ghostly glasses clink.
Our life's a cycle between here and there.
We believe the dead still love us, still care.
We're not frightened on the Day of the Dead.
We pull out a chair, say, "Sit down," instead.
We make cookies, but ghosts just eat the smell,
Leaving more for me, and that's truly swell.
We bake cakes and pies, whip up candy, too.
Oh, I *love* sharing with the dead. Don't you?

PRAISE-THE-CHICKEN DAY
—OR ELSE

A great chicken scientist, Harriet the Hen,
Built herself a time machine to travel back to when
Chickens lived free in the wild, eating what they would.
(Prehistoric chickens ate nothing very good.)
So the wise hen traveled back to the mid Jurassic,
The golden age of dinosaurs—giant and fantastic.

The great chicken scientist was then nearly stomped,
Nearly sat on, flattened, crushed—oh, dear—almost chomped.
So our feathered heroine hopped ahead in time
To the year 2050, which for chickens was sublime.

There a breed of super hens, engineered by science,
Rule the planet Earth entire, no one dares defiance.
Chickens there do what they will, only what they wish,
And are never cooked and served as a dinner dish.
With the biggest brains on earth, smart as smart can be,
Hens produce no eggs for breakfast, dinner, lunch, or tea.
When a chicken passes by, humans all must bow,
(Bow also to the biodesigned supersmart new cow).

Now kind Harriet returns to warn of what lies ahead,
In a future filled with dark years of feathered dread.
So we must establish soon a day to honor hens,
To prove that we mean well before their reign begins.
And if you think otherwise, you are in grave error—
One day you will live under gruesome chicken terror.

DIWALI BY GOLLY

Diwali, Hindu festival of lights,
Brightens each city and town for five nights.
In every window of homes great and small,
Clay oil lamps wink, shadows dance on the wall.
On every outside step a lamp burns, too.
Fireworks paint the sky—a heavenly view.
Small boats with candles float on the river,
Honoring Laksmi, the fortune giver.
This goddess of riches and generosity,
Visits lucky homes during Diwali.
I hope good Laksmi visits all of you.
And by golly I hope she visits me, too.

NATIONAL BOOK WEEK:
Why Paper Tigers Are the Preferred Breed

I don't want *Harry Potter* chiseled on big heavy rocks,

Or recited by the cuckoos in sixteen cuckoo clocks.

I don't want Lemony Snicket writing on smelly socks,

Or with purple chalk on blocks and blocks of sidewalks.

I don't want to read a story writ in blood—too gory.

A tale told on 10,000 T-shirts would truly bore me.

A Western yarn branded on the butts of broncos bucking

Would be hard to read while I was leaping, ducking.

Writing on scrolls (like toilet-paper rolls) was once the rage,

But I much prefer to read stories on the printed page.

Reading a tale tattooed upon a tiger's tongue

Might be exciting if you don't mind dying young.

HOLIDAY, HOLINIGHT

Too few holidays celebrate the night,
So we must do something to set this right.
New Year's Eve, Christmas Eve, Halloween, too,
Are happy enough but are still too few.
Let's honor the moon, let's honor the stars,
Celebrate lightning bugs caught in glass jars,
Praise all the creatures who come out at night—
Bats, moths, owls and . . . some that give us fright:
The gumfing, swizzing, cat-eating red toad;
The fibbus groon living under the road;
The mimsy, slithy old serpentine yurp
That eats boys and girls with many a slurp,
Loves ears and fingers but will not eat toes,
For some reason yurps cannot abide those.
Applaud the flying, fanged, green gabbagoo,
The clawing, snapping, bloodsucking blue boo.
And now tip your hat to the spickelspeen,
Meaner than vipers, oh, even *more* mean,

That eats those poets caught all unaware,

And flosses its teeth with ropes of their hair.

Spickelspeen, Spickelspeen, it nightly cries,

As through the pearly moonlight it flies.

"Spickelspeen, Spickelspeen!" Hey, who said that?

"Spickelspeen, Spickelspeen!" Hey—(splat, splat, splat)*

* Editor's Note: This unfinished poem was completed with three words
provided by the attorneys for the poet's estate, following a three-day
creative meeting with thirty-one experts in contemporary verse. Credit for
these three words must not be given to the absurdly incautious poet, who
should not have gotten so caught up in the sound of his own rhymes that
he forgot the risks of his profession.

THANKSGIVING TURKEY
DRESSED IN HAND-ME-DOWNS

One year we raised our turkey

From chick up to the table.

But when we had to ax him,

Not one of us was able.

We ate rice and beans instead,

And gave him a nice warm bed.

We bought him toys, clothes, and boots.

Soon the turkey put down roots.

"He's a sweet child," Mother said,

As she tucked him into bed.

Father said, "He looks just like

Your dad's brother—Uncle Mike!"

We're brothers of a feather

In both good and foul weather.

In shoes he'll sometimes wobble.

But then sometimes I gobble.

He hurts my ears every time he sings.

And he can't fly, though he has two wings.

Yet I'm thankful for him, yes I am.

He's nicer than my brother, the ham.

Yes, we once raised an Easter pig. Wow.

We should *never* raise a Christmas cow.

THE FIRST DAY OF WINTER

We like winter cold and white.

We like every snowy night.

We like to skate, like to sled,

Like to wear wool socks to bed,

Make snowmen, have snowball fights.

We like all the Christmas lights,

Like hot chocolate by the fire,

Like our too-cool ski attire.

We like flu, we really do,

Like to cough and cry *Achoo!*

We like sneezing, we like snot.

We like snot an awful lot!

We like slipping on the ice.

Breaking bones is really nice!

Yeah, winter can be a bummer.

But there's sunburn in the summer.

Bees will sting you in the spring.

Autumn's when the school bells ring.

Give me flu and give me ice.

Snot or not, winter is nice!

THE SHORTEST DAY OF THE YEAR

Shortest day of the year is in December.

It was so short I can hardly remember

Whether I got out of my bed or forgot,

Whether I took a shower—or maybe not.

I must admit to a degree of surprise

That the sunset so quickly followed sunrise.

I might not have had time to feed our good cat

If he had not spit at me, clawed, screeched, and spat.

I couldn't do my homework—not enough time.

I barely found a minute to write this rhyme.

No time for any chores, or to make my bed,

Because the day raced away, flew past, it fled!

I think I deserve admiration, not blame

For finding ten hours to play a video game.

CHRISTMAS EVE

Did you see reindeer on the roof?

I did, I did, and I've got proof.

I climbed up high, I slipped, I slid.

I almost fell and broke my lid.

I almost tumbled loop-de-loop.

And stepped right in some reindeer poop.

I've got the proof, I do, I do!

See, it's right here on my shoe.

CHRISTMAS DAY

Tom got sports gear, Mary got ice skates.

Ben got a robot that spins and vibrates.

Jack got an electric train with a red caboose.

Heather got a tame, fancy, saddled moose.

Harry got some action figures, Bill got more.

Sue got a puppy that peed on the floor.

Jamal got a ball, Inez got some books.

Myrtle got a turtle with prehistoric looks.

A frisky little pony went to Leroy in Dubuque.

Nicky got a fruitcake—oh, but it made him puke.

Sammy got a sports car big enough to ride.

Lisa got a surfboard to slide along the tide.

Jose got a guitar, Jimmy got a set of drums.

Ramona got bright jewelry to wear on her thumbs.

And the world got a message centuries ago

That love, faith, and peace are the way to go.

UP-IS-DOWN DAY

Today, oh today, is Up-Is-Down Day,
When all is confused in every way.
You arise with a most funny feeling
That your bed is up high on the ceiling.

You stroll the ceiling and then down the wall,
Pass through the doorway, out into the hall,
Where yet again you are safe on the floor,
Though nothing is quite the same as before.

Up is down also means left is now right.
So much has changed since the previous night.
Backward is forward and now yes means no.
Today low is high, today fast is slow.

You climb fast backward up to the downstairs,
Where in the kitchen your mother declares,
"Table's on the wall, window's on the floor.
You don't want bacon? Then say you want more."

Sweet rolls are sour, eggs come with jelly.
None of this sits too well in the belly.
Toast jammed in a glass, orange juice on a plate.
"Hurry, you're early," Mom says, but means "late."

Dad comes for breakfast by way of the sink.
At this spectacle you don't even blink.
He throws out the cereal, and then eats the box,
With tasty dry milk. On his hands he wears socks.

Dad says "hello," which of course means "good-bye."
He would say "how" if he meant to ask "why."
He leaves for work through the refrigerator,
Steps over the bear, who's a grumpy hibernator.

Tonight there will be a big Up-Is-Down party,
To which all the guests must be sure to be tardy.
Cooks will play music and the musicians will cook.
Guests come to be seen, but no one will look.

The window in the floor shows a snowy June day.
The dog puts on his boots to go outside to play.
The snow looks as hot as thick steaming stew,
So you'll stay indoors while the TV watches you.

Now we will celebrate in this Up-Is-Down way
To remind us that any ordinary day
May seem sometimes dull, but is in the main
Just what we need if we are to stay sane.

KWANZAA

When it began, "Kwanza" had just one "a."
But in '66, on the first Kwanzaa, they say,
Seven children wanted to hold signs on the stage
Spelling out the word. So some clever sage
Said, "Let's just add an extra 'a,' one more letter
To include the seventh child." It's always better
To include than exclude, which we all would agree.

Kwanzaa would be even more fun, if you ask me,
Even more fun, festive, and outrageously fine,
Had nine hundred more kids wanted to hold a sign.
Yes, another nine hundred of the letter "a"
Would require us to add one more Kwanzaa day,
Because one entire day would be fillable
Just to pronounce the final syllable!

NOT THE STUFF OF HOLIDAYS

Benny found a strange booger in his nose.

Sally found some weird stuff between her toes.

Harlan found green wax deep inside his ears

That smelled so bad it brought the dog to tears.

While all this is interesting in its way,

It's not worth declaring a holiday.

Dean Koontz is a world-famous author whose novels have sold more than 250 million copies in thirty-eight languages. He has numerous *New York Times* adult best-sellers, including his most recent, THE FACE. Dean Koontz is also the author of the children's books THE PAPER DOORWAY and SANTA'S TWIN. He lives in southern California. Visit his website at www.deankoontz.com

Phil Parks is also the illustrator of THE PAPER DOORWAY and SANTA'S TWIN. A freelance artist, his other work includes limited-edition books, magazine illustrations, and private commissions. He lives in Clarkston, Michigan.

INDEX